Eric Hayden understands true revival. He also understands that true revival usually comes when God's people pray for the gift of the Spirit biblically and passionately. This book should be commended to church leaders the world over. It is both clear-headed and warm-hearted.

John H. Armstrong
President, Reformation & Revival Ministries
Carol Stream, Illinois USA

PRAYING FOR REVIVAL

Eric Hayden

Christian Focus
Reformation & Revival Ministries

ISBN 1 85792 686 2

Published in 2001
by
Christian Focus Publications, Geanies House,
Fearn, Ross-shire, IV20 1TW, Great Britain
and
Reformation & Revival Ministries, Inc.
P.O. Box 88216
Carol Stream, Illinois 60188 USA

Cover design by Owen Daily

Contents

Part 5
Prayer for CORPORATE revival:
God's people and nations

Part 6
Prayers for the REVIVAL OF GOD'S WORK

Epilogue

FOREWORD

The name of Eric Hayden is well-known in Britain – particularly in Baptist and generally in evangelical circles – as a faithful pastor, an able preacher, and a talented writer. He is considered an expert on C.H. Spurgeon, in whose steps he followed as pastor of the Metropolitan Tabernacle in London.

There are those who interpret Finney's maxim: 'Revival is nothing more than the right use of the appropriate means' to imply that such a movement of the Spirit may be arranged at a time of man's choosing, by meeting certain conditions. Undoubtedly, any time an individual Christian or any body of Christians decides to live up to the light already possessed a measure of reviving is the result. But this is far from the scope of a movement offered in Scripture and exemplified in the records of history.

Eric Hayden has written upon Revival in the higher sense of a sovereign act of God, brought about by the Spirit of God through the Word of God among the people of God. He has written from the depths of feeling of British Christians who are not so appeased by the intoxication of evangelistic and pastoral 'success' as is the case in Canada and the United States where superorganization and technique have robbed their practitioners of the sense of need of a sovereign move of the Holy Spirit which would revive the Church and awaken the people through a thoroughgoing repentance.

As one who has dedicated energies to the collecting and retelling of the mighty acts of God in the past (including the immediate past), I commend this treatise on Praying for Revival as an application of the models and patterns and examples of Scripture, borne out by history.

J. EDWIN ORR.

Introduction

Revival depends upon the sovereignty of God. He sends a spiritual awakening where, when, and upon whom He wills.

Yet a study of the revivals of the past, in Scripture and in the history of the church, reveal that God's sovereign act always followed hard upon the prevailing prayers of His people. The central condition of 2 Chronicles 7:14 is 'If my people . . . shall . . .Pray. . . then will I heal their land.'

How our lands need 'healing' today, for we are living in days of spiritual destitution. The twentieth century has been in the main a deplorably irreligious century. The Bible has been neglected by Christians; the Church has been forsaken by many, and multitudes desecrate the Lord's Day. Any vestige of Christianity in so-called 'Christian countries' like Britain and America is an inheritance from a previous generation. Very few living today know of revival at first hand.

Once again we must turn to prayer. Yet never having experienced revival on a large scale we need to say: 'Lord, teach us to pray.'

It has been estimated that there are 650 definite prayers in the Bible, 450 of them followed by recorded answers. Thirty-five of these prayers are revival prayers, that is, taking those with revival images, metaphors, similes, such as 'quickening', 'awakening', 'turning', 'raining', 'flooding', and so on. These thirty-five can be conveniently grouped into the sections within the compass of this book.

During the 1904-05 revival in Wales, a man travelled from Wiltshire, England, to Wales to learn the secret of the revival from Evan Roberts. Roberts said to him: 'My brother, there is no secret. Ask and ye shall receive!' Matthew Henry, the renowned Bible commentator, wrote: 'When God intends a great mercy for His people, the first thing He does is to set them a-praying.' May God the Holy Spirit so move among His people in these last days that we are again set 'a-praying'. As a result may revival come upon the church of God and upon the world around; God's people within and the unsaved without. May this little book be instrumental in encouraging groups, even twos and threes, to meet regularly to pray for revival, basing their prayers upon the Scriptural pattern.

The scheme within Scripture is: Prayers revealing the **Need for Revival;** prayer for **a Vision of Revival;** prayers to the **Sovereign God of Revival**; prayers for **Personal Revival**; prayers for the **Corporate Revival of God's People**; prayers for **National Revival**; and prayers for the **Revival of God's Work**.

Part 1

Prayers revealing the NEED for revival

1

WHY? and WHERE

'And Gideon said unto him, Oh my Lord, if
the LORD be with us, why then is all this
befallen us? and where be all His miracles
which our fathers told us of, saying, Did not
the LORD bring us up from Egypt? but now the
LORD hath forsaken us, and delivered us into
the hands of the Midianites' (Judges 6:13).

Gideon had the courage to ask a question openly
that many are afraid to ask. We have become so
complacent, so used to the spiritual decline all
around us, that we do not ask, 'Why should these
things be?' We talk of half-empty churches. If
they were half-empty then they would be half-
full and many are much less than half-full. To
the preacher they represent a dead 'timber yard'
from the pulpit: row upon row of empty pews,
especially at the front of the church so that nobody
seems to be sitting 'under the sound of the
gospel'.

Conversions are few and far between. The
meetings for prayer and Bible study are poorly
attended. The Lord's **Day** has become a **half-day**
and most of the church members have become
'oncers'.

Why is this? What has happened? What has become of all the 'pulpit giants', spiritual men who could command a vast congregation?

Well, this situation is not new. It has happened time and again, and time and again God has brought revival under such men as Jonathan Edwards, George Whitefield and John Wesley.

Notice that Gideon prayed to the Lord's **angel**, yet it was the Lord Himself who answered. Sometimes in the Old Testament the angel of the Lord stood for a personal manifestation of God Himself and that may have been the case here.

The first lesson, then, to learn, in praying for revival, is to 'take it to the **Lord** in prayer' as the hymnwriter puts it. He alone has the key and the power to solve the problem. The answer to our desperate plight is not in men or methods but in God alone. 'Oh my Lord', cried Gideon.

Next, Gideon told the Lord of **the desperate situation**: 'delivered into the hands of the Midianites', a nomad people, the first to use the camel in their plundering raids. They were past masters at creating havoc and descended upon their enemies like a plague of locusts. God's people in Gideon's time were reduced to living like trapped animals in caves because of them.

How honest Gideon was with God. 'Preacher's count' is an expression for those who can always count more heads in a congregation than anyone else! Many ministers when asked 'How is your work going?' reply in vague terms such as, 'Oh, not too bad; we're seeing some blessing' (although the blessing is not specified) and so on. If we were as honest as Gideon we would specify the 'all this', the loss of everything dear to us; the helpless feeling of being 'forsaken' or cut off, as if God had removed His presence from us.

Naturally it is humiliating to have to confess all this. Our sinful pride makes us loath to do it. So we try to bolster things up and make out that the situation is not as bad as it appears on the surface.

Finally, Gideon reminded God of **the dynamic possibilities**: 'all these miracles'. What were they? The crossing of the Red Sea, the Passover night, the crossing of Jordan, the water from the rock, manna in the wilderness, the giving of the Ten Commandments, the capture of Jericho, and so on. 'Up out of Egypt' is specifically mentioned for it was the most wonderful of them all and most appropriate for an illustration of revival. God's people first went down into Egypt because of famine. There they became oppressed. Even when told that the Land of Promise awaited them they did not want to leave! How difficult it is to get a church to see that there is something better for them than the dryness they are experiencing. How difficult to stir up zeal and enthusiasm in place of complacency. How difficult to get them to see the need of revival.

2

Divine Insomnia

'Awake , why sleepest Thou, O Lord? arise,
cast us not off for ever. Wherefore hidest Thou
Thy face, and forgettest our affliction and our
oppression? For our soul is bowed down to
the dust: our belly cleaveth unto the earth.
Arise for our help, and redeem us for Thy
mercies' sake' (Psalm 44: 23-26).

God's people in the Old Testament not only felt
their need for revival when national religion was
in decline, but when they personally felt destitute
within. If they had known it they could have
prayed the revivalist's prayer: 'Lord, send a
revival, and begin with me.' That is how the
Psalmist felt, although here he is personifying the
people of God and praying on their behalf, for
their need of revival is so great.

Verses 13, 14 and 17 reveal his deep concern
and understanding of the situation: 'Thou makest
us a reproach to our neighbours, a scorn and a
derision to them that are round about us ... Thou
makest us a byword among the heathen, a shaking
of the head among the people ... all this is come
upon us' (the last phrase being reminiscent of
Gideon's 'all these').

The burden of the Psalmist's prayer is for God to 'arise' and 'awake', but God does not sleep, He only seems sometimes to be asleep. 'The God of Israel neither slumbers not sleeps' – **Divine Insomnia** as it has been called.

In times of spiritual decline it does seem as if God is asleep and needs arousing. It seems as if He has cast His church to one side. It seems that He is absent from the battlefield when the forces of evil seem bent on destroying the church. So it seemed to the Saviour on the cross: 'Why hast Thou forsaken me?' But He was not utterly forsaken. God was still working His purpose out.

In spite of our empty pews and other outward signs of spiritual decline God is aware of our plight.

This is daring language by the Psalmist, and this is the kind of language that prevails with God. When the disciples cried 'Carest Thou not that we perish?' then Christ came to their rescue. Of course He cared; He knew their plight; He came to their aid at just the right time.

No, this is not a cry of accusation but a despairing enquiry.

In his prayer the Psalmist describes the need. It was twofold: physical and spiritual. 'Our soul is bowed down' (spiritual) . . . 'our belly cleaveth unto the earth' (physical). So man's need today is twofold and only a spiritual revival can set us free from the sinful spirit of materialism that prevails in the world and the Church.

The Psalmist was being ruthlessly honest. God's people were as low as they could get – right down in the dust. So we must humble ourselves and 'prayer must be heartfelt prayer . . . from unreality O set us free.' We must confess our worldliness, our materialism, our love of position and possessions; our love of academic attainments in the ministry instead of a sound knowledge of the Word of God. We must admit that we have relied on personality rather than spirituality. We must confess that all our reliance upon 'gimmicks' has failed to attract people to Church and to Christ. For only then can we go on to pray: 'Arise for our help . . . redeem us.'

Finally, note how the Psalmist's prayer was short yet comprehensive. These verses take only twenty-five seconds to pray aloud. The Psalmist comes to the point in simple, clear, urgent language.

In the County of Salop, England, there is a hill called 'The Wrekin'. It is a landmark for miles around. The Salopians who live beneath the hill have a saying that when people take a long time getting to the point in their conversation 'they are going all round the Wrekin.' So often our prayers are not efficacious because we go all around instead of straight to the point.

We need the daring of the Psalmist; the simplicity of the Psalmist; the fervency of this man of God, as we make our need of revival known to the Help of the helpless.

What kind of prayers do we offer up? Indefinite? Petitions couched only in general terms? Or do we do as the Psalmist did and think back to what God had done in the past in order to find encouragement for the future? – 'We have heard with our ears, O God, our fathers have told us, what work Thou didst in their days, in the times of old' (v.1).

We may not have had the privilege of living in revival times, but we can still talk with those who have been through such a manifestation of the Spirit of God; we can still make a serious study of the revival of history. This will have the twofold effect of emphasising our need for revival and spurring us on to pray more regularly and fervently for another revival.

Once again the Psalmist prays with the knowledge that revival is all of the sovereignty of God: 'For they got not the land in possession by their own sword, neither did **their** own arm save them: but **Thy** right hand, and **Thine** arm, and the light of **Thy** countenance, because **Thou** hadst a favour unto them' (v. 3).

The 'O God our help in ages past' of the hymnwriter is our only reliable source of help today and for future days.

3

Conversion and Re-conversion

'Turn us again, O God, and cause Thy face
to shine; and we shall be saved. O LORD God
of hosts, how long wilt Thou be angry against
the prayer of Thy people? Thou feedest them
with the bread of tears; and givest them tears
to drink in great measure. Thou makest us a
strife unto our neighbours; and our enemies
laugh among themselves. Turn us again, O
God of hosts, and cause Thy face to shine;
and we shall be saved' (Psalm 80:3-7).

There are five outstanding points in this prayer
for revival that was prayed by a man who knew
the dire need for revival.

He begins with a plea: 'Turn us again, O God,
and cause Thy face to shine.' 'Turn' is a favourite
word in the Old Testament for revival. The
Psalmist was not praying that God would turn
circumstances and situations. His prayer was
'Turn us.' An old religious cliché is: 'Prayer
changes things.' True, but prayer also changes
people! It is people who are the real hindrance to
revival. Even Christians can be stumbling blocks,
so the path to spiritual renewal is blocked. And
since we cannot turn ourselves (as we could not

at conversion – for it is 'by grace you are saved') it is the sovereign God who must turn us around.

What sort of turning was the Psalmist indicating? What sort of turning do we need? It is a turning from carnality to spirituality; rebelliousness to willingness; sinfulness to sanctification.

If we continually ask the question: 'What sort of persons ought we to be?' then we shall continually pray to be turned around. The world so easily comments: 'Look at him, her – he, she goes to church and is no different, no better for it.' Then, if that is a criticism of us, we need to be turned.

First, He turns us, then He turns to us! What a sight we then behold: 'Who dwellest between the cherubims!' (v.1). What glory, what majesty confronts us. That is true revival, when God manifests His presence among His people and to His church.

The plea is followed by **a question**: 'How long wilt Thou be angry?' We often think God withholds revival because God is angry with His church and its sins. He is grieved by our sins, but He is angry **with our prayers!** He is a prayer-hearing and a prayer-answering God who loves to listen to and delights to answer our petitions. How then can He be angry? The Psalmist was writing of prayer that was unacceptable to God because of its formality, its presumptions, and its being offered with iniquity in the heart. When prayer becomes just vain words, with no real feeling, then God is angry with us.

Next comes a **twofold statement**. The first is: 'Thou feedest them with the bread of tears.' Their food had become unpalatable because it was saturated with salty tears. Every meal was like a mournful funeral feast. The tears had made their drink saline too, and they were drinking not only cordial but copious draughts of tears ('In great measure', literally a Hebrew expression for four times as big as usual).

The reason was not the havoc caused by their enemies but that caused by themselves. After all, if God is angry with our prayers, how can we pray without distress and sorrow of heart?

The next statement is: 'Thou makest us a strife ... our enemies laugh among themselves.' What a sorry state for the people of God, to be continually ridiculed by the world. How similar today, in the news media, papers, magazines, television, sound radio – the parson is always good for a laugh or some silly cartoon. Comedians can always raise a laugh by telling a funny story about a parson. And what strife there is within the church: at deacons' meetings, church meetings, trustee meetings, board of governors, and so on. Some of it would never be countenanced in a worldly business, but in the Church of God it is allowed to go on and fester.

In the Acts of the Apostles we find the revived Church is held in awe and reverenced.

Then comes **a plea** again, and this time a repetition of 'Turn us.' 'Turn us again' prays the Psalmist. In the face of all that the world is doing to God's people he can only repeat his plea, but now with renewed emphasis. The first plea was to God; the repeated plea is to **the God of hosts**, the God of angelic powers.

The Psalmist knows that he is praying to a God of unlimited power. Nothing can withstand Him. His wording implies that the hosts of heaven are marshalled, in military array, ready to do battle and to do God's bidding.

What have we to fear? Let us pray on and look up, not looking at our weakness but at His strength. Declining statistics may dismay or deter some, but the true believer, concerned and burdened for revival will see all the Divine resources at the disposal of the Church.

Finally, note **the consequences**: 'we shall be saved.' Not salvation from sin, but real wholeness and liberty in the Lord. When the Church is revived it becomes a healthy Church, freed from all the besetting sins that clog our progress for the gospel.

In Liberia the missionaries talk of converts 'turning their hearts to the Lord.' So the unrevived believer and corporate Church must be turned again to the Lord.

4

Rejoicing in God!

'Turn us, O God of our salvation, and cause Thine anger toward us to cease. Wilt Thou be angry with us for ever? Wilt Thou not revive us again: that Thy people may rejoice in Thee? (Psalm 85: 4-6).

This revival prayer begins with similar wording to Psalm 80:3-7. The great difference is that the Psalmist has now seen his first prayer answered and he has experienced revival – 'LORD, Thou hast been favourable unto Thy land' (v.1.)

Revival in the past should always inspire us to greater prayer for a present and future awakening. We are, after all, only asking God to do what He has done before.

Again we need to note that the request is for a re-direction: 'turn us.' Help us face and follow another way; the way of sincere repentance and reliance upon Sovereign power.

And again the Psalmist is conscious of Divine anger, but not this time because of wrong praying, but because of wrong living. He does not want to see the divine anger 'drawn out to all gener-ations.' How sad it is that only the very old in most of our churches today have ever witnessed, experienced or been in contact with someone who has actually been through a time of refreshing from the presence of the Lord. The young know nothing about revival from firsthand experience. Surely we don't want our children and grand-children to be so spiritually impoverished, and so we must pray for a turning-again that they may witness revival in their time.

The word used in this prayer for 'revive' does not mean bringing back from the dead, that is resurrection. Revival is fanning into a flame a dying spark. When a church is dead then the Spirit has been grieved and withdrawn His presence; there can be no revival there. But where a small spark remains, where a faithful, praying remnant remain, then the Holy Spirit can fan that into a flame again.

The crux of this prayer, however, is: 'Revive US again', not 'Fill our empty pews, give us bigger congregations and more numerous converts' – these are the outcome of revival, not revival itself.

Revival is first of all personal, God dealing with us as individuals. When He does that, then the consequence is great rejoicing: 'Thy people ... rejoice in Thee.' C.H. Spurgeon once said: 'a genuine revival without joy in the Lord is as impossible as spring without flowers, or daydawn without light. If either in our own souls or in the hearts of others, we see declension it becomes us to be much in the use of this prayer, and if on the other hand we are enjoying visitations of the Spirit and bedewings of grace, let us abound in holy joy and make it our constant delight to joy in God.'

Joy in God! God is the Psalmist's great emphasis throughout this prayer. We could not do better than kneel by our bed, with Bible open at this prayer, and take it phrase by phrase and make it personal, admitting that we have not experienced the blessings our forefathers knew; then confess anew our need of re-turning; and finally cry out to God for a Divine visitation.

There are conditions, however. All God's promises are conditional. Verse 8 sets out the condition: 'Let them not turn again to folly' or as *The Living Bible* rightly translates it: 'If they will only stop their sinning.'

This Psalm also reveals the social outcome that true revival always exhibits: (v.12) 'Yea, the LORD shall give that which is good, and our land shall yield her increase.' In Old Testament times religious revival always affected the State of the land or nation. Again *The Living Bible* makes the sense clearer: 'Yes, the Lord pours down His blessing on the land and it yields its bountiful crops.'

Harvest time was the criterion by which national prosperity was judged in those days. Today revival would affect our economics in all fields: strikes, go slows, devaluation, restricted imports and exports, exorbitant taxation, the continual rise in the cost of living.

Revival is the solution to the believer's state of backsliding, his coldness of heart, his lack of zeal and enthusiasm. Revival is the solution to the church's lack of evangelistic witness and joy in worship. Revival is also the solution to the needs of the world, economic, political and inter-personal.

5

A Pattern Prayer

'Wilt thou not from this time cry unto me,
My father, Thou art the guide of my youth?'
(Jeremiah 3:4).

This brief revival prayer is a pattern or model prayer given by God Himself to the prophet, similar to how the Lord Jesus Christ later gave a pattern prayer to His disciples.

First, in verse 2 of the chapter we note the need for revival: 'lift up your eyes unto the high places.' The country was in an immoral state. The religious declension is described under the figure of harlotry.

In return for sincere repentance, and in answer to this prayer, God would give 'showers' and 'latter rain', verse 3 – two common metaphors for revival.

Now God could have treated them like Sodom and Gomorrah with fire and brimstone rained down upon them. But here He is more merciful; by withholding rain, which resulted in no growth, no swelling of the grain, they had to realize their utter dependence upon Him as the Sovereign God. Spiritual dependence should always make God's people look around, at the state of the churches and also within (the state of our own sinful hearts). Then we should look up, with a dependent look at the faithful God of past eras.

To help Jeremiah look up this prayer was given. Although short, definite and to the point, it contained all that was necessary for such dire straits.

Many of the most beneficial prayers in the Bible are 'telegram' or 'arrow' prayers: 'Help, Lord'! 'Lord, save me,' 'Carest Thou not that we perish', 'God be merciful to me a sinner.'

There is no wordy, eloquent prayer that is more effective than a short fervent one.

'From this time' means literally 'at this time' – this time of weakness, evil, wickedness, devastation, decline. So at this present time in the world's history, now is the time for short petitions to the point, pleading with God the Father to bestow His favour upon us in another worldwide spiritual awakening.

Note that it was a 'cry', that is a heartfelt cry, a cry of anguish or despair. A cry, the noise made by a young child, not the polished sentence of an adult. A child in pain cries or a baby in need.

There are two important principles involved in this short prayer. First, we must notice **the One petitioned**: 'my Father.' God was reminding Jeremiah of his particular relationship with Himself. The prophet was not to imagine that he was coming into the presence of a despot; there was no need of fear or trembling. It was to be a child-father relationship, or a relationship based on love. The Christian is one who can address God as 'Abba' – father (literally Daddy or Dada), the first word a baby speaks. So in our prayers we come with filial love, to a Father who is compassionate and wants to do the very best for us.

Dr. Campbell Morgan tells of a deacon in one of his early churches who used to go 'all round the world' in his prayers and never ask for anything definite. One day a voice called out, 'Call Him Father and ask Him for something!' He hears and answers the momentous and the most trivial of our requests. 'Bless our church', 'Bless the missionaries' – these are too indefinite.

Next, note **the petition itself**: 'Thou art the guide of my youth.' The more correct rendering is: 'Thou **wast** (past tense) the guide of my youth.' It is a reminder to Jeremiah that what has always been so He ever will be. Ebenezer and Jehovah-jirah: hitherto and henceforth the Lord will provide – 'great is Thy faithfulness.' He is the same today as yesterday.

Because God has sent revival again and again so we may go on praying believingly and expectantly while we watch and wait for Him to work.

Some commentators say that 'guide' here should read 'husband'. If so, then a special relationship is emphasised once again. God as Father is One who protects and provides for His children; as husband He is also provider and protector of His bride, and more, He is lover and companion.

Revival begins in our own hearts when we begin to experience this special relationship we have with the Lord. 'My beloved is mine and I am his' – that is the perfect relationship between God and children that forms the basis of spiritual revival. What a pity that John Newton's hymn has often been altered. Originally it read:

> 'Jesus! my shepherd, husband, friend,
> My prophet, priest, and king;
> My Lord, my life, my way, my end,
> Accept the praise I bring.'

If we want revival we must recapture the relationship we once had at, and soon after, our conversion, asking: 'Where is the blessedness I knew when first I saw the Lord?' We must get back to our first love with all its enthusiasm and zealousness. 'Turn' is used in verses 7 and 14 and 'return' in verse 22. *The Living Bible* puts it: 'Come home, come back.' Revival begins when returning prodigals come to the Father's house and live again within the special relationship that is there.

PART 2

A prayer for a
VISION of revival

6

Opened Eyes

'LORD, I pray Thee, open his eyes, that he may see'
(2 Kings 6:17).

Dr. Alexander McLaren said: 'The revelation of
the angel guard around Elisha is the important
part of this incident, but the preliminaries to it
may yield some instruction.' They certainly do.
They reveal first the great need for revival in
Gideon's day. There had been a partial one in
that the worship of Baal had been relinquished,
but the calves at Bethel and Dan had been
retained.

These 'preliminaries' also reveal that there had
been much spiritual work put in by this 'quiet
prophet', Elisha. Quiet, but 'more to Israel than
an army' it has been said.

Everything seemed against Elisha as
everything seems to be against the progress of
the Christian church in a Communist or
materialistic society. Dothan was a small isolated
place, easily surrounded, and a night attack (with
its element of surprise) a sure way to victory. The
scheme failed, however, because Gehazi rose too
early one morning and discovered the besieging
army.

35

Gehazi and Elisha make an interesting contrast. Gehazi stands for the nominal, status quo Christian; Elisha the longing-for-revival believer. Gehazi, like most nominal Christians, soon fell into despair. Elisha saw beyond the present material facts and saw spiritual, heavenly realities. 'Fear not,' he said (v.16), for he saw that the sovereign God was in control.

Note that the prophet did not pray to God to provide a means of deliverance – he saw that it was already there. His prayer was that another might see them as he saw them. Revival is not something that can be arranged for a certain date; it cannot be organized; but we can lift up our eyes and see all the resources of God at our disposal, available whenever we want to use them. Our prayer must be that others might see these divine resources and come to rely on them.

What a sight Elisha saw: a flaming ring of hosts of heaven; horses and chariots; and fire – a common symbol for revival in God's Word.

How our eyes are blinded to God's provision for His Church today! Like Gehazi we are earth-bound creatures and think only in terms of men and methods, better publicity, more visual aids, modern translations of the Bible, and so on. But these are mere trifles when compared with the Divine resources. Like Gehazi we need our spiritual cataracts removed from our eyes.

This sight was given in answer to prayer:

'LORD, I pray Thee, open his eyes, that he may see.' That was the prayer. This was the answer: 'And the LORD opened the eyes of the young man; and he saw.'

The false cults grasp one another by the shoulder and try their salesmen talk on the doorstep, saying, 'Now will you see it; now will you grasp the doctrine I am trying to put across to you.' They fail because they do not believe in the mighty eye-opening work of the Holy Spirit. When argument fails; when eloquence fails to appeal; when there is no emotional response, then it is time the Holy Spirit removes the scales from the eyes.

What a difference it would make to our churches if only we had a company of Elishas who constantly prayed for the eyes of others to be opened to the power of the sovereign God to bestow revival. Perhaps we must begin in a personal way and pray: 'Lord, open my eyes that I may see, for I have been blind, bewildered by men, indifferent to the plight of the Church.'

The final important thing to notice is that Elisha prayed for a **young** man's eyes to be opened. How we need the young (who have never seen, experienced or perhaps not even read about revival) to catch a sight of what God can do! Sometimes the older church members are too set in their ways to change. Then let us concentrate on the next generation and pray for their eyes to be opened, that they might not be content with the nominal, formal religion of their parents but yearn and long for great outpourings of the Spirit of God upon the churches. They need to know that it is not 'pop' groups strumming their guitars, religious dance and drama, and all the rest of the modern 'crazes' that will bring revival. This is only 'candy floss' religion, effervescent Christianity. These are just gimmicks that help the church to keep its head above water. Revival is the unleashing of the floodgates of heaven, the bestowal of the illimitable resources of God upon the people of God. First, however, we must pray that He will open our eyes to the infinite possibilities.

PART 3

Prayer to the
SOVEREIGN GOD
of revival

7

Showers of Blessing

'We acknowledge, O LORD, our wickedness, and
the iniquity of our fathers: for we have sinned
against Thee. Do not abhor us, for Thy name's
sake, do not disgrace the throne of Thy glory:
remember, break not Thy covenant with us. Are
there any among the vanities of the Gentiles
that can cause rain? or can the heavens give
showers? art not Thou He, O LORD our God?
therefore we will wait upon Thee: for Thou hast
made all these things' (Jeremiah 14:20-22).

Perhaps the most common metaphor in Scripture
for revival is rain showers of flood waters. The
later hymnwriters carried on the same picture
language: 'There shall be showers of blessing'
and 'Lord, I hear of showers of blessing', being
two of the most common examples.

The prophet Jeremiah used the same metaphor
for revival as he acknowledged the sovereignty
of God in revival in his prayer.

The important point to note in the context of
this prayer is that God had told the prophet
explicitly **NOT** to pray: 'Pray not for this people
for their good' (v.11). But Jeremiah was burdened
so much that he disobeyed God and poured out
his soul in prayer.

What a need there was for showers of revival blessing in Jeremiah's time, just as there is the wide world over today. The wickedness and the iniquity of the fathers is pin-pointed in this chapter, and the sinfulness of the whole generation of God's people (vv. 10,14,19b).

The need was also a longstanding one, physical as well as spiritual ('sword and famine', v.16). The enemy had conquered God's people and famine was keeping them cowered. So depleted and weakened were they that they could not bury their dead! So it is often with the church today. Christian fellowships are starved of sound doctrine; there is a dearth of true gospel preachers; the world has encroached into the life of the church; the onslaught of Higher Criticism and Modernism has damaged the church's reliance upon the Scriptures as being infallible and verbally inspired.

The prophet first confesses that he has been looking in vain from wrong sources for help: 'the vanities of the Gentiles' and 'the heavens' (that is, the Baal rainmakers). Matthew Henry comments that 'only the God who answers by fire can send water too!' So, too, today we often try wrong methods, relying upon so-called 'revivalists', or hastily organised half-nights and whole-nights of prayer, as if revival is a kind of 'penny-in-the-slot-machine', instead of the result of action by the sovereign God in His own time and way.

Jeremiah is thus forced to confess his sole dependence upon the sovereign God of revival: 'Lord'!

This Lord is a covenant-keeping God. That, comments Charles Haddon Spurgeon, is always an argument to be used in prayer. God is One who can never go back upon His word and must fulfil His promises to His people.

Then He is the Creator Lord: 'Thou hast made all these things' (v. 22). What things? The natural order of the universe around us, especially the cycle of moisture, drawn up from the sea, released on the land, running again to the sea. He created the system and He controls the system. He can send or withhold the rain.

Thus Jeremiah is content to wait for God's own good time: 'Therefore we will wait upon Thee.' So must we. It cannot be emphasised too often that we cannot work revival up or pray it down. We must pray, but we must learn to wait for the 'sound of a-going in the tops of the mulberry trees', the moving of the Spirit of God among His people. Our prayer must be:

My times are in Thy hands,
Whatever they may be;
Pleasing or painful, dark or bright,
As best may seem to Thee.

We cannot do anything else than pray to, then rely on, the sovereign, covenant and creator Lord

God, from whom **all** blessings flow. We must affirm the truth of the hymnwriter:

> There shall be showers of blessing:
> This is the promise of love;
> There shall be seasons refreshing,
> Sent from the Saviour above.

> There shall be showers of blessing
> Precious reviving again;
> Over the hills and the valleys,
> Sound of abundance of rain . . .

As we pray, 'Lord, send a revival and begin with me,' so we must continue:

> Lord, I hear of showers of blessing
> Thou art scattering full and free –
> Showers the thirsty land refreshing;
> Let some droppings fall on me –
> EVEN ME!

PART 4

Prayers for
PERSONAL revival

8

Settling for Less

'Behold now, Thy servant hath found grace in Thy sight, and Thou hast magnified Thy mercy, which Thou hast shewed unto me in saving my life; and I cannot escape to the mountain, lest some evil take me, and I die: Behold now, this city is near to flee unto, and it is a little one: Oh, let me escape thither, (is it not a little one?) and my soul shall live' (Genesis 19:19-20).

Lot is not pictured in a good light in this passage of Scripture. He is a man in need of spiritual revival. He has achieved position and prominence and power in Sodom, but to the detriment of his spiritual life.

Visited by two angels, in order to save him from the Sodomites, he offers his own daughters to the crowd that they might have their way with them. The angels save Lot and his daughters by sending blindness on the Sodomites. The one redeeming feature is that Lot tried to warn his sons-in-law, giving them an opportunity to escape.

The angels persuade Lot and his wife to leave Sodom before Divine destruction falls. They must go to the mountains. Lot, however, has an alternative escape route, preferring man's choosing to God's appointing, and so prays this prayer.

In the prayer we first notice **Lot's estimate of himself**: 'Thy servant.' The words are not strictly true, for the first mark of a servant is obedience and Lot would have taken God's way of deliverance. Lot was disobedient, wilful, stubborn, obstinate. Revival can never come to an individual or church in that condition.

Like Paul, we must be willing to become Christ's bond-slaves if we are to experience revival. 'The servant is not above his Lord.' Christ must have the pre-eminence, He must come first in everything. We must want to obey Him in all things, being ready and willing to run His errands and go and do what He wants.

Next, we note **Lot's esteem of God**: 'Thou hast magnified Thy mercy.'

God had showed mercy to Lot in the past, preserving his life, saving him from many perils. A few moments previously the angels had pulled him back into the house from angry crowds. Then, while still lingering, he was taken out of the city to safety.

In a similar way, how merciful God has been through the centuries. The revivals of history prove how God has continually magnified His mercy towards us. The church has been delivered again and again from spiritual decline. This was not due to our merit but to His mercy.

Then notice **Lot's evasion of God's will**: 'I cannot escape to the mountain.' God's way of escape was a hard route. It often is. It was going to be a long trek, a strenuous uphill march. There were no means of escaping the rigours of the journey. So spiritual revival is a costly road, costly in time, prayer and money. Like Lot, when we consider the cost we are tempted to be content with lesser alternatives, a lower level of spirituality. 'Come up higher' is the Lord's word to us.

Then we must note **Lot's enthusiasm for an alternative**: 'This city is near.' How enthusiastic Christians can get over alternatives to revival as they imagine them to be: gigantic evangelistic crusades with their many spiritual 'casualties'; coffee bars and discos; visitation evangelism; tract distribution; the grouping of churches under team ministries (all good in themselves), but certainly these are no alternative to revival. These other things are the ordinary, regular ongoing work of the church while awaiting for the Sovereign God to act through revival.

Finally, we must note Lot's expectation of personal revival: 'My soul shall live.' First, Lot thought only of saving his own skin. Then he realized that the soul is more important than the body. True revival is life in the soul ('Quicken me' was the frequent prayer of the Psalmist). The world and the devil do all they can to bring deadness into the soul of the Christian and the life of the corporate fellowship, the church. Materialism causes difficulty in praying; it hinders meditation and study of God's Word; it limits our witnessing.

This is a prayer to be pondered over frequently. It reminds us of the tragedy of settling for less than God would love to bestow upon us. Lot was going to be content with the tiny town of Zoar instead of the high mountain peak. Revival is living in the uplands in the rarefied atmosphere of God Himself, not living a restrictive existence in the cities of the plains.

9

The Spring of Him Who Prayed

'And (Samson) was sore athirst, and called on
the LORD, and said, Thou hast given this great
deliverance into the hand of Thy servant: and
now shall I die for thirst, and fall into the hand
of the uncircumcised?' (Judges 15:18).

The need for revival is often illustrated by dryness or barrenness in Scripture. The advent of
revival, by contrast, is illustrated by water and
fruitfulness. A desert of a thirsty person is thus
transformed into a garden of a revived saint.

The Philistines had been trying, without
success, to capture God's servant Samson. Three
thousand of God's people tell us that by fighting
he is rebelling against their conquerors and that
he should stop before the consequences become
too disastrous. They have a plan: they will deliver
him as a prisoner to the Philistines. Samson goes
along with their scheme, planning to break free
and do much harm. He does it, by the Spirit of
the Lord and with the jawbone of an ass. His arms
become like fire (another revival metaphor) and
he kills a thousand of God's enemies.

This, of course, was thirsty work and he felt
after it that he was dying of thirst, and so he

prayed a prayer for personal revival. In his prayer he first of all **acknowledged what God had done**: 'Thou hast given this great deliverance.'

'To God be the glory' should always be the keynote of revival praying. Samson had done the killing but strength had come from the Lord.

The slain were placed 'heaps upon heaps' (v.16) and so God's goodness to His people could be assessed. They could 'count (their) blessings.'

Looking back we can study the revivals of history and see the 'heaps' of blessing, the rent heavens, the spiritual rain sent down upon the church.

Next, in his prayer Samson **acknowledged his own portion**: 'Thy servant' (as did Lot). Samson was a man of great strength but he used it in the service of the Lord. All that he was he dedicated to the Lord. The servant must be subservient and willing to serve with all readiness, humility, obedience and, if need be, servility. These are the requirements for all God's people before revival can come. God 'resists the proud'; He can have no dealings with those who are puffed up with their own importance and self-reliance.

Then Samson **acknowledged his dependence upon God for the future**. Samson knew that unless God dealt with his raging thirst he would weaken and become useless, falling into enemy hands and dying a cruel fate.

Note that Samson felt weak after a great

victory! It is often so. Our Lord later felt virtue go out of Him after a miracle. Ministers of the gospel are weakest on Monday morning, especially if they have experienced great spiritual blessing on the previous day, the Lord's day. Success should never make us self-confident, but feeble and afraid. It should make us all the more dependent upon God for future blessing and victory in the spiritual life.

How wonderfully this prayer was answered. God supplied Samson with water from the ass's jawbone, or from the ground below the bone, the spring bursting forth through the bone (v.19). The result was: 'his spirit came again' ... 'he revived'. Revival is when our spirit comes again, like an athlete who receives his 'second wind' during a long distance race. The Hebrew word for 'spirit' is the same as for 'wind'. When the wind of God fills the believer's soul then he is in a revived state.

He **revived!** That is, Samson regained his spent energy. His waning strength returned. His weakness left him. He recovered his desire to do further exploits for the Lord. That is what the church needs today, a recovery of apostolic zeal; a New Testament enthusiasm for the extension of Christ's kingdom. At the present time we are enfeebled, powerless, a laughing stock to the world. When revived then we shall be able to pull down the strongholds of Satan.

No wonder Samson called the place where he was revived 'En-Hakkore', that is, 'The spring of him who prayed.' Are there any En-Hakkores in our lives, hallowed spots where prayer for revival have been answered and we have felt anew the infilling of the Spirit of God? Maybe it is some private room, some lonely hillside; perhaps the shore by a lake, a convention tent, our church – any place where we felt the need of the Spirit, prayed to the sovereign God of revival and He heard and met our hour of need.

10

Best of Men for the Worst of Times

'O LORD my God, hast Thou also brought evil upon
the widow with whom I sojourn, by slaying her
son?... O LORD my God, I pray Thee, let this child's
soul come into him again' (1 Kings 17:20, 21).

The answer to this prayer is in three words: 'And
he revived.' Elijah, who has been called 'the best
of men for the worst of times', prayed on behalf
of the widow's son for the personal revival of
her child.

The widow, first approached by the prophet
in his time of need (hunger), soon found her own
need supplied. 'The LORD my God' is the phrase
Elijah used twice in his prayer, thus emphasising
his faith in the sovereignty of the Almighty.

First, the prophet expresses his personal faith
in this sovereign God: 'O LORD *my* God.'

LORD infers dignity, honour and majesty. The
English word is represented by three Greek words
in the New Testament and nine in the Hebrew of
the Old. It was the term that inspired awe and
reverence in the one using it. It made one think
of God as creator, controller, sustainer, provider
and redeemer.

In view of the widow's need the prophet could

call Him by no other name. On a bed lay a dead child, only the Lord of all life could help.

Our twentieth century Christianity, by contrast, is flippant and superficial. The name of God is tossed about on television and radio, and blasphemy is all too common. God's name should be held in great reverence, especially by those who pray 'Hallowed be Thy name.'

Man has become deified by the scientists and God has been dethroned by the God-is-dead theologians! Revival tarries until Christians recapture their faith in the sovereignty of God, the great emphasis of the Calvinists and Puritans.

Next, Elijah states his **perplexity** in a strange situation: 'Hast Thou also brought evil upon the widow with whom I sojourn, by slaying her son?'

This is the great problem that has confronted and confounded men throughout all ages: a good-living person upon whom comes some unexpected calamity. It is the problem of the Book of Job. Why should she be penalized when she lived such an upright life? So today there are those who say they are religious, they sit in church and not in a public house; they do not take drugs and are not contemplating divorce – and suddenly sorrow and calamity come into their lives, either affecting them or someone dear to them.

How difficult it is to understand the untimely death of small children! For the aged and infirm it is often a 'blessed release' but for one who has hardly begun along the road of life . . . !

What a parallel this is with the declining state of the church today. Often the gospel is faithfully preached by the pastor and yet a modernist church around the next corner can be full to overflowing.

Neither problem can be understood with our human, finite minds. We shall have to wait for the 'Fair schoolroom of the sky' for the solution to our problems. In the meantime we must pray on.

So the prophet makes a **powerful plea** to his sovereign God: 'O Lord, my God, I pray Thee, let this child's soul come into him again.'

Once more Elijah uses 'Lord', and the personal pronoun 'my'. Then he adds 'I pray Thee', the same word that he used of his own need to the widow. The word means 'I beseech' and has the idea of incitement and entreaty behind it.

The situation is desperate and so desperate measures are needed and desperate language must be used. So the spiritual situation is desperate today: the spiritual darkness and deadness upon so many of our churches means that we must pray desperately. Time is short. The Lord is coming again. There are many Christless souls going to a lost eternity. We must pray in desperation for the revival of the church that the church might bring life to these lost souls.

Notice how the widow could hardly believe

her eyes. Elijah had to stress: 'See, thy son liveth.' Matthew Henry comments: 'See, it is your own (son) and not another'. So it will be when the church is revived. Our now-doubting minds will hardly believe the difference. At the moment we base our ideas of a few score or maybe a hundred or two souls saved. But we shall be astounded when we see the effect of a real heaven-sent revival upon the church. We shall begin to doubt if it is the same church that we have worshipped in and belonged to all the previous years!

One thing we can be sure of: that widow woman never again doubted the word of the Lord. Once we have experienced revival we shall never doubt again the power of prayer and the power of the sovereign God to send revival.

11

Scriptural Steps to Revival

'Create in me a clean heart, O God; and renew a right spirit within me. Cast me not away from Thy presence; and take not Thy holy spirit from me. Restore unto me the joy of Thy salvation; and uphold me with Thy free spirit' (Psalm 51:10-12).

Psalm 51 is known as one of the great Penitential Psalms, that is, it contains a deep sense of sin and a profound desire for forgiveness. Such is the only way to true fellowship with God and true joy in the heart. The Psalmist here shows how personal revival results from taking certain, simple steps.

First, he asks for a **clean heart**: 'Create in me a clean heart, O God.' Having confessed in the previous verses his sins he now desires a new heart devoid of all evil. Only God can provide this, for it is a divinely creative work. The Psalmist was not praying for an old heart to be 'doctored up', patched, or made to look like new. He was asking for a spiritual heart-transplant. The same God who made heaven and earth is the One who can give new, clean hearts.

Our thoughts of personal revival must be similar to those we had before our conversion.

We discovered then that we could not patch up the rags of our own righteousness. No! we had to 'put on Christ.' So with revival. The deadened heart cannot be revived by our own efforts any more than turning over a new leaf, it is a new life!

Next, the Psalmist prayed for a **renewed spirit**: 'Renew a right, persevering and steadfast spirit within me.' The idea is of standing firm in the hour of temptation. Revival in the soul guards against backsliding. The Psalmist does not want to live as in verses 1-5. A new heart deserves something better, a life of victory. Well, the same God who gives the new heart can give the necessary steadfastness moment by moment to combat all the wiles of the devil and the pressures of the world and the flesh.

Third, he prays for an **established fellowship**. 'Cast me not away from Thy presence.' This is the picture of the eastern courtier banished from the king's presence because he has incurred the royal displeasure. The revived Christian, by contrast, lives in the presence of the King continually, experiencing that fellowship which is established by the Holy Spirit through the Son.

Sin always results in broken fellowship with God: 'Your iniquities have separated between you and your God.' The hymnwriter asks the question: 'Where is the blessedness I knew when first I saw the Lord?' An old preacher commented:

'Right where you left it brother!' Yes, right where we left it when we fell into sin. As a leper was banished outside the city gates to the leper colony, so the sinner is banished from the presence of the Lord, for 'nothing that defiles can enter in.'

Next, the Psalmist asks for **a guaranteed power**: 'Take not Thy Holy Spirit from me.' Was he thinking of Saul's great tragedy when the Holy Spirit departed from him (1 Sam. 16:14)? Without the Holy Spirit we are unable to combat temptation, overcome sin, witness, testify. We cannot do these things in our own strength.

Now the Holy Spirit departs when grieved or when quenched. How carefully then must we speak about Him. If He departs then we have lost the only available source of power for the Christian life.

The Psalmist's next petition is for **restored joy**. 'Restore unto me the joy of Thy salvation.' What a lot of joyless Christians there are in the world (coffee-pot faces, spiritual 'indigestion' sufferers). How different from Paul's injunction to the Philippians to 'rejoice .. always!'

How happy we were when first converted! Joy came through sins forgiven, through losing our guilt and the shame and the penalty of sin. Revival is when this initial joy is restored constantly; we thus live daily as if each day is the day of our conversion.

This is what attracts the man in the street, when

he sees joyful Christians even when in adversity.

Finally, the Psalmist prays for **spontaneous enthusiasm**: 'Uphold me with Thy free spirit.' Various explanations of 'free' are given by Bible commentators: 'willing spirit,' 'spirit of alacrity'. As there is no 'Thy' in the ancient manuscripts we must suppose that the Holy Spirit is not meant here. The Psalmist is asking for the spirit of consistency, spontaneous enthusiasm, for his next words are: '**Then** will I teach transgressors Thy ways; and sinners shall be converted unto Thee.'

How difficult it is to persuade some Christians that they should be soul-winners, even though Scripture insists that 'he who wins souls is wise' (read it backwards: 'He that is wise wins souls'!). Spurgeon discovered after his first convert had been won that he felt like a deep sea diver coming up with a pearl!

When revival comes to the heart of Christian people it will be the most natural thing in the world for them to go with enthusiasm to seek the lost. They will 'gossip' Christ like the early Christians. Revival turns tongue-tied believers into eloquent evangelists quicker than anything else.

12

Maintain the Spiritual Glow

'My soul cleaveth unto the dust: quicken Thou
me according to Thy word' (Psalm 119: 25).

'Quicken' or make alive is a frequent Old
Testament word for spiritual revival. Sometimes
it was used for an actual revival. Sometimes
it was used for an actual resurrection from the dead
(Psalm 71:20) when such qualifying words are
added as 'from the depths of the earth.'

In Psalm 119 it is the spiritual revival after
declension that is meant, for the soul has been
'cleaving to dust', that is, it has got as low as can
be.

'This is not the prayer of the unconverted,'
one commentator says, for 'he was alive; he was
a spiritual man, or else he would not have asked
for life, for dead men never pray 'Quicken me'.'
It is a sign that there is life already there when a
man is able to say 'Make me more alive, O Lord.'

So the regenerate man needs his spiritual life
regenerated, made anew, each day if he is to live
in a revived state. As fire must have fuel and air,
so the believer must pray for God's quickening
Spirit in the life of the soul. The advice given to
young converts always used to be: 'Maintain the

spiritual glow' and regular 'Quiet Times' of Bible reading and prayer were considered essential for this.

The Psalmist's brief prayer is in three parts:

First, **he describes his condition**: 'My soul cleaveth unto the dust'.

All of us are 'of the earth, earthy'. The Psalmist had reached a position in which he found it difficult to 'set his affection upon things above'. He had become earthbound.

Just as the natural man is an earthbound creature and can only travel in outer space with special equipment and machines, so the spiritual heights are not our natural element spiritually. The natural man 'cleaves' or adheres, clings to, sticks to, is fastened to the dust, the earth or world. For the Jew 'dust' meant ashes or rubbish.

How often Christians adhere to the rubbishy things of life, to the detriment of their spiritual lives: to magazines, cheap novels, obscene films, plays, television shows. Dust, through static electricity, often clings to clothing as small pieces of tissue paper cling to an ebony ruler that has been rubbed with silk. In the same way we allow the things of the world to cling to us and only the Lord can 'quicken' us by releasing the magnetism.

Next, the Psalmist **declares his need**: 'Quicken Thou me.'

Having described his need, and knowing that

there is something better in store for the people of God, the Psalmist declares his need.

'What manner of persons ought we to be?' is Peter's important rhetorical question. We know in our heart of hearts that we ought to be better than we are. We also know that God is able and willing to make us more like Himself.

The trouble is that some have been taught to believe that 'We've received all there is at conversion' or 'We've received it all at a subsequent 'second blessing'.' 'Still there's more to follow' says the old hymn and hymnology is in tune with theology at that point. The consecration of a believer, his sanctification, is something that goes on moment by moment, daily.

Finally, the Psalmist **depends on the Divine promise**: 'According to Thy Word.'

Charles Haddon Spurgeon always used to insist when preaching about prayer that 'prayers that plead promises guarantee success'! God is a covenant, promise-keeping God.

Now the Psalmist had only a small portion of the Word of God to plead from. We have a complete Bible containing hundreds, thousands of promises. Many of these promises are to do with revival, personal revival, so let us plead them in our praying, especially this one for new life, for it is 'according to Thy word.'

The way the answer came is very instructive. The Psalmist pleaded for a fulfilment of God's

Word. God used His word to bring life to His servant's soul – verse 93 says: 'I will never forget Thy precepts; for with them Thou hast quickened me.'

Many Christians think revival is going to be a certain sort of **experience.** Certainly experience plays an important part in revival: an experience of the sovereignty, majesty, glory and excellence of God as a Person. Others think that revival is fulfilling certain **conditions.** Yes, there are conditions to be fulfilled: humility and prayer ('if my people shall humble themselves . . .'). But revival is often when God speaks to us through His word, simply and plainly, feeding us until our spiritual hunger is satisfied. As we read, hear and study His word we see our faults and failings and want nothing more to do with them. We see that there is something more in the Christian life, something we have not yet possessed, and so by faith we claim them, allowing the Spirit of God, the Author of the Word, to teach us. There's nothing like the Word of God for revitalizing, for reviving our spiritual life, for the Word is both milk and meat, two essential items of diet for two different stages of development – babies and grownups. It is also 'honey', which is good for thrombosis, sore throats, and even burns! So the Word of God is suited to all our spiritual ills; so it makes us live in a revived state.

13

Strong Crying With Tears

'Hear my prayer, O LORD, give ear to my supplications: in Thy faithfulness answer me, and in Thy righteousness. And enter not into judgment with Thy servant: for in Thy sight shall no man living be justified. For the enemy hath persecuted my soul; he hath smitten my life down to the ground; he hath made me to dwell in darkness, as those that have been long dead .... Quicken me, O LORD, for Thy name's sake: for Thy righteousness' sake bring my soul out of trouble' (Psalm 143:1-3, 11).

The Psalmist frequently felt in need of revival but he never prayed more revealingly, fervently and appealingly than in these verses.

First, he acknowledges the Almighty as a prayer-hearing and a prayer-answering God: 'Hear ... give ear ... answer me.' The difference between 'hear' and 'give ear' is that hear is 'pay attention' and 'give ear' is 'apply one's ear to', a much stronger expression. So there is mere **prayer** (asking for this and that), and **supplication** (which is more fervent and intensive and asking special favours).

There is no request like that for revival to be

bestowed so sure to catch the divine attention. Who can cry for it, knowing its cause and effect upon the individual, the church and world, in a semi-individual, manner? It is like asking for fire or flood so we should be 'on fire' when we pray and ready for 'waters to swim in.' And because God is 'faithful' and 'righteous' He must hear and answer. 'Faithful' is a mild attitude; 'righteous' is a stern, severe characteristic. Both are on the side of the man who prays for revival: the goodness and the severity of God.

It has been well said: If in prayer **we** have great **intention**, then God gives greater **attention!**

Next, the Psalmist acknowledges his own subservience and insignificance.

'Thy servant . . . no man living (can) be justified,' he says.

God is the Judge of all mankind, every living being. How insignificant the Psalmist feels as he comes with his own needs. God is all-seeing. His eyesight is as acute as His hearing. He knows the secrets of every soul. None can stand guiltless before this awesome, righteous, holy God. He knows all and must pronounce judgment upon all.

How subservient the Psalmist is – 'servant', that is, one who is in the pay, the home of another, and under the command of another. He cannot live pleasing himself, doing what he likes. Thus the servant can only come into his master's presence in humility, relying on his master's goodness and generosity, his kindness and fairness. So the Psalmist comes to God, entirely dependent upon Him.

Third, he acknowledges a threefold need: 'Persecuted . . . smitten down . . . in darkness as dead.'

Note that his soul was persecuted, not his body. Revival is always a spiritual matter, not simply empty pews and pulpits devoid of pulpit giants. There are churches in Communist countries, their bodies are persecuted, but spiritually they are very much alive.

God's life is in the soul and Satan is the 'enemy of souls'. He does attack bodies, for Paul's affliction was due to the devil buffeting him. But Satan's real target is the believer's soul and spiritual life.

'Smitten down' means crushed. Note the direction: downwards, not heavenwards. That is always the direction Satan strikes. We sometimes talk about being 'knocked sideways'. Satan's attacks are always in the opposite direction to heaven. Lack of revival is when we are smitten down; revival is when we are lifted up.

'Darkness as death' – not darkness as in sleep. This darkness is of a permanent nature rather than transitory. The darkness is like death, and Satan is the Prince of Darkness. It is his job to see that we become downcast and disconsolate and driven to despair so that we exhibit no life, no movement.

Finally, he acknowledges the Almighty's power to revive and restore: 'quicken . . . bring out of trouble.'

The Fount of all life alone can give life and light. The Psalmist sees nothing in himself that is deserving of God's favour; he can only pray 'for Thy name's sake'. Revival is always a vindication of the name and glory of God, and God vindicates Himself and His church 'for His righteousness sake', so that men may see how right and just He is in caring for His beloved people.

In righteousness God will lift up, revive, restore troubled people to tranquillity. John Trapp's comment is: 'I can bring my soul into trouble, but Thou only canst bring it out.' By worldliness, neglect, listening to Satan, we get into soul trouble. God alone can bring us up and out into the blessings of revival.

C.S. Lewis comments: 'The first eleven verses were written in a strain that brings tears to the eyes.' So we should be tearful as we see our own plight and the plight of the church. But inability means His ability to revive. Here then is a prayer that is 'strong crying with tears.'

14

A Voice from the Depths

'I went down to the bottoms of the
mountains; the earth with her bars was about
me for ever: yet hast Thou brought up my
life from corruption, O LORD my God. When
my soul fainted within me I remembered the
LORD: and my prayer came in unto Thee, into
Thine holy temple' (Jonah 2:6, 7).

Jonah has been disobedient to the divine
commission to preach to Nineveh. He has evaded
his duty and taken a ship to Tarshish. In a storm
at sea he is thrown overboard but in the Lord's
mercy he is swallowed by a big fish and after
three days and nights coughed up on a beach alive.
He has another chance to fulfil his commission
to preach repentance to Nineveh. In the 'whale's'
belly he offers up a prayer of thanksgiving for
the preservation of his life. From the tenses used
he also includes future deliverances which he
anticipates.

Like the other people who pray for personal
revival in God's word Jonah first realizes **his
desperate condition**: 'I went down to the bottoms
of the mountains; the earth with her bars was
about me for ever.'

The sperm whale can descend to great depths. Jonah was taken down to the sea bed, to the very foundations or roots of the mountains. He found that the land of the living was shut out by dark, unseen conditions of the deep.

The Moody Institute of Science's film *Voice of the Deep* destroys the myth that the depths of the sea are silent. The hydrophone (an underwater microphone) reveals that fish talk to one another, even in the uninviting, murky depths of the sea bed. So the unrevived church or believer lives in dark and depressing conditions, cut off from the power and presence of God, missing out on the joy of the Holy Spirit. The New Testament church, by contrast, knew life, light and love. They lived on the mountain tops and not in the depths. Their faith was fluid and not static; their worship was not formal and icily regular. The gifts of the Spirit were manifest and easily recognizable. They were not like drowning birds but like free birds.

Next, Jonah resorts to **a delightful consolation**: 'I remembered the LORD.'

Although he felt weak and helpless and near to death, he did the one thing that needed doing, he prayed to the Lord.

His personal danger reminded him of the need of personal revival. He remembered the Lord's mercy, power, wisdom, compassion, and covenant-keeping nature. In the words of the hymnwriter: 'In thy weakness, in thy peril, Raise to heaven a trustful call; Strength and calm for every crisis Comes by telling Jesus all.' Or in the words of another shipwrecked sailor: 'Weak as you are, you shall not faint, Or fainting, shall not die, Jesus, the strength of every saint, Will aid you from on high.'

Jonah's help came from on high – 'Thy holy temple'. His despairing cry went right to heaven's Holy Place, the throne of God in heaven. Spurgeon comments: 'His prayer was not drowned in water, not choked in the fish's belly, neither was it held captive by the weeds that were about his head, but it went up like an electric flash, through waves, through clouds, beyond the stars, up to the throne of God.'

The result was personal revival. He was brought up from the depths and out of darkness. He was restored from fainting and spiritual weakness. He lived again and could face the wickedness of Nineveh.

What a prayer! One commentator says: 'Jonah had no prayer-book (God the Holy Spirit can put more living prayer into half-a-dozen words of your own than you could get out of a ton weight of paper prayers).'

Jonah's prayer was not notable for its words. The fish's belly was not the place for eloquent phrases, nor for long-winded orations. His prayer was shot by the strong bow of intense desire and agony of soul, and, therefore, it speeded its way to the throne of the Most High.

No wonder Jonah became a type of Christ for many Bible commentators. His three days and nights in the fish's belly prefigured the three days and nights of our Lord in the tomb after Calvary. Jonah had a resurrection experience similar to our Lord's. It was by the Spirit of God that Jesus was raised from the dead. And it is by that same Spirit that we are raised to revival life from the depths, darkness and spiritual decline so prevalent among believers today.

May Jonah's voice from the depths lift us up to the heights of communion and fellowship with the sovereign God of revival.

Part 5

Prayer for
CORPORATE revival:
God's people and nations

15

'The Pursuit of God'

'Now therefore, I pray Thee, if I have found
grace in Thy sight, shew me now Thy way,
that I may know Thee, that I may find grace
in Thy sight: and consider that this nation is
Thy people' (Exodus 33:13).

Great Britain once used to be known as 'the
people of the Book', for the Bible was read in
every home and quoted by politicians in
Parliament. Scripture was appealed to as a final
authority. Now, alas, the Bible is neglected or
ignored and the Lord's Day and His houses of
prayer desecrated and left well-nigh desolate.
Only a revival of church and nation can change
such a dreadful situation.

There are several prayers in the Bible for the
revival of God's people and God's power is
unchanged to bring about revival in any nation,
east or west (crippled by communism or
materialism).

God had led His people out of Egyptian
bondage. He had provided for them in the
wilderness. The ten commandments and other
ordinances had been given. The Tabernacle had
been constructed and the priesthood appointed.

The stage was surely set for national prosperity. But the laws were soon broken and true religion became pagan idolatry. The only hope was revival and for that Moses prayed.

He did not pray, however, until after the people were repentant. So it must be with us. We must 'repent from (turn from) our wicked ways' before He will 'heal our land.'

Moses then ascended Sinai and prostrated himself before the Lord in prayer. How burdened he was. He remained in prayer for forty days. How little we are burdened by contrast!

He first uses his **influence** with God: 'If I have found grace in Thy sight.' Moses had not worshipped the golden calf. He had tried to keep the wayward to a straight and narrow path. Surely for those endeavours God would look favourably on his petitions. So we must endeavour to live lives unspotted from the world, so that God will look upon us with favour.

Next, Moses uses **inquiry**: 'Show me now Thy way.' Literally he was saying, 'Make me to know Your ways', a request to know Divine principles, the way in which God deals with persons, nations, granting prosperity and averting adversity. Only as he understood could he lead the nation in God's way. Our need today is for the nations of the world to have leaders who will continually seek to know and to do God's will, not just 'toeing the party line.'

Third, there was **identification** prayed for: 'That I may know Thee.' First, personal revival, before corporate and national revival. Only as Moses became personally revived could he influence others. The world does not take much notice of the unrevived Christian.

Moses' petition prefigured that of Paul's: 'That I may know Him' (Philippians 3:10). Some want to know how to speak in tongues, others how to heal the sick – in fact they are seeking gifts rather than the Giver. We need to know HIM and the power of His resurrection. Dr. A.W. Tozer in his book *The Pursuit of God* tries to stimulate readers to increase in a hunger and thirst after knowing God. He follows the thought of the prophet Hosea: 'Then shall we know, if we follow on to know the LORD.'

Next comes **indulgence**: 'That I may find grace in Thy sight.'

Moses wished to be so identified that all that he said and did would be considered in a favourable light, God indulging His grace and favour on behalf of him and the nation. This is also New Testament doctrine: 'Ye ought to walk and to please Him who hath chosen Him to be a soldier' (2 Tim. 2:4).

How long is it since we walked like that, trying at each step of the way to please God? The result is always revival in the soul.

Finally comes the note of **insinuation**:

'Consider that this nation is Thy people.'

What a daring approach to God in prayer! Moses was saying, in effect: 'Since my people are really Your people, they should not be left without the inspiration of Your presence.'

In one sense we cannot pray this petition for neither Great Britain nor America are the chosen people of God (unless we belong to and believe in the 'British Israel Movement' which has no Scriptural grounds for its beliefs). In another sense we can and must pray it, for God is the Creator of all people and every nation needs the inspiration of His presence.

Moses' prayer was abundantly answered: 'My presence shall go with thee.' Revival comes to a nation when the presence of God is realized in the midst. When God is seen in industry, commerce, politics, in national and international affairs, then revival has come. Moses insinuated that it must be so. God could not forsake them because of His special covenant relationship with them. So Christians burdened for revival must daringly place the responsibility of revival upon the sovereign God of revival, the creator of all mankind.

16

Sepulchre or Shrine

'And now, O LORD God, the word that Thou
hast spoken concerning Thy servant, and
concerning his house, establish it for ever, and
do as Thou hast said. And let Thy name be
magnified for ever, saying, The LORD of hosts
is the God over Israel: and let the house of Thy
servant David be established before thee' (2
Samuel 7:25, 26).

The history of revivals shows that national revival
frequently follows revival in the church. The
church in a revived state is able to influence
politics, industry, commerce and social life. When
sin is rife in the nation then the need is for the
church to pray for revival so that the nation can
be transformed.

Thus it was in David's day. David was at first
forbidden to build the Temple as he was a man
of war and not a man of peace. When wars had
established the kingdom, then the temple plan was
approved by Nathan.

The initial divine reluctance was easily
understood: 'a gorgeous stone temple might
easily become the sepulchre, rather than the
shrine, of true devotion.' So it did, and so it has

often been with the church. That is why so many churches might be described as 'spiritually dead' today, and that is why many nations are also spiritually dead.

Nathan told David that the temple would be built by his successor. This, however, did not prevent David praying for the success of the venture. So, although we might be disappointed and not see revival in our lifetime, that should not prevent us praying for it.

Here in David's prayer we have the exception to the rule. We have noted that all these revival prayers are **short** ones. This one, by contrast, is **lengthy**. David begins with thanksgiving in verses 18 to 24. Verses 25 and 26 contain definite depictions built on the promises within the previous verses. The key words are: 'Do as Thou hast said'. As we have noted before, there are no unanswered prayers if we plead God's precious promises. It is not presumptuous to take God at His word, it is an act of real faith. 'If we ask anything according to His will, He heareth us.' So we must 'stretch our desires to the width of God's promises' as one commentator puts it. And He has promised: 'Times of refreshing **shall come** from the presence of the Lord.'

There are two secrets in this part of David's prayer, in particular the way David speaks of God and then about himself.

First, David refers to God with **frequency and**

variety. There is a threefold calling on the name of God, each time using a fresh name. An old deacon once told his Pastor to listen carefully at the prayer meeting to the prayers of his people. 'Those continually growing in grace will use more and more names and titles of God, not just "O Lord, O Lord, do this, give us that." ' How true!

In the first place David refers to the Almighty as 'O LORD God.' That phrase implies a personal God, the great I AM, the new name given to Moses.

The One to whom all prayers for revival should be addressed is 'O LORD God'. Prayer is **to** God, **through** Christ, as prompted by the Holy Spirit. 'O LORD God' implies that we are addressing the One who is the same 'yesterday, today and for ever'. It reminds us of His unchanging nature and power. What He has done for our forefathers He can do for us.

Next, David addressed his prayer to the 'LORD of hosts', the God with a heavenly army (angels at His disposal). This phrase emphasizes His majesty and His might, that He is omnipotent. No church or nation can withstand Him if He should deign to send an outpouring of His Spirit in revival power.

Finally, David uttered the words 'God of Israel', that is, the God of His own chosen people, the God of national revival. Chemosh was the god of Moab; Dagon the god of the Philistines; but Jehovah was the God of Israel. He had given them victory in battle; He would be with them as a nation as they built the temple.

When Great Britain stood alone in the Second World War, in the dark hour called 'Dunkirk', God performed a miracle and kept the English channel calm for three days for all the evacuating little ships. He was then our God. Now our gods are sport, pleasure, money, gambling, and materialism. Only when we are willing to return to Him will He send revival upon us.

Next, David spoke of himself with **frequency and humility**. Once in every verse from verses 25 to 29, and twice in verses 27 and 29, David uses the words 'Thy servant'.

As we have seen before, servant is a term of absolute subjection. It was used by kings when referring to their court servants. David, though a king, uses it of himself, for he is subject to the King of kings. So the believer who desires revival must look upon himself, as Paul did, as the 'bond slave of Christ.'

There is one final secret. David prayed that God's name might be 'magnified for ever.' He did not pray for worshippers to fill the temple. He did not pray for the reputation of the temple to be enhanced. Revival praying is praying that God's name might be glorified and His reputation vindicated.

17

Showers of Blessing – 2

'When heaven is shut up, and there is no rain,
because they have sinned against Thee; if they
pray toward this place, and confess Thy name,
and turn from their sin, when Thou afflictest
them: Then hear Thou in heaven, and forgive
the sin of Thy servants, and of Thy people
Israel, that Thou teach them the good way
wherein they should walk, and give rain upon
Thy land, which Thou hast given to Thy people
for an inheritance' (1 Kings 8: 35, 36).

The privilege and responsibility of building the
Temple passed from David to Solomon. It was
built in silence (1 Kings 6:7) but opened with
ringing and royal tones in prayer, a prayer that
was 'lofty, spiritual and saturated with Scripture.'
The House of God was dedicated and the people
of God blessed.

In the middle of the prayer, Solomon delivers
a poignant appeal for national blessing and
obedience. Verses 35 and 36 sum up his request
that Israel as a nation shall be spiritually revived.
He uses the common metaphor of drought and
rain for spiritual revival.

First, Solomon confesses the nation's

condition: 'Heaven is shut up'. This is a most eloquent phrase to describe the condition of drought and dryness, the barrenness and dearth of spirituality prevailing at the time. Being agricultural people they depended on rain to soften the rocklike soil. Psalm 63:1 aptly describes this condition: 'A dry and weary land where no water is.' No ploughing and sowing till rain comes in sufficient quantity. The farmer depended on the 'former' rain for softening the soil ready for ploughing and sowing, then the 'latter' rain for swelling the grain and fruit ready for reaping. In between would be the intermittent showers, but the former and the latter rains were more copious.

How dry and barren the Christian church is when through carnal members, unspiritual leadership, the church takes on a worldly air. So with the nation when it becomes materialistic, and when immorality, vice, violence, drug-addiction, demonstrations and discrimination become the order of the day.

Next, Solomon confesses his reason for the drought: SIN! – 'Because they have sinned against Thee.'

Note the 'against thee'. We can sin against others and do so when we steal, gossip, commit murder, but since these are also breaking divine commands, ultimately all sin is against God, the great Lawgiver. The essence of sin is wrongdoing against His holy name and nature, His righteous laws and commands. All unconfessed, unforgiven sin acts as a barrier, separating the sinner from a holy God. 'Righteousness exalts a nation but sin is a reproach.'

Thirdly, Solomon sets out in his prayer the conditions of revival. They are threefold:

First, pray (this being in keeping with 2 Chronicles 7:14 – 'If my people pray . . . '): 'If they pray toward this place.'

The individual believer, who knows spiritual dryness and barrenness, needs to turn more frequently to prayer. So nations must learn to observe more days of humiliation and prayer than those held during a time of national crisis. But while our nations persist in desecrating the Lord's Day and neglecting His House of prayer, there can be no real revival.

The second step is to 'Confess (His) name'. God must be publicly acknowledged at all levels of national life. He must not be left out of committees and subcommittees, Parliaments and Senates. He must be pre-eminent in politics, industry, commerce, education, and the social life of the nation.

Then they had to 'turn from their sin'. There had to be real, true, genuine repentance, not just a feeling sorry. Turning is the hardest part in repentance. It is easy to pay lip service to God and join in a General Confession at a church service, but to give up those things that have become a personal and national disgrace (lotteries, greed and graft, vice and violence, sex and pornography, gambling and alcoholism), that is real turning, the kind of repentance that God requires before He can send revival.

Fourthly, Solomon prays for the coming revival: 'Then hear Thou . . . forgive . . . and give rain upon Thy land.'

This picture of rain upon the restoration of the land is a favourite one in the Old Testament. 'And I will cause the shower to come down in his season, there shall be showers of blessing' (Ezekiel 34:26). 'I will pour water upon him that is thirsty, and floods upon the dry ground' (Isaiah 44:3). The natural and literal in Scripture often has a spiritual parallel or counterpart. The outpouring of rain for the prophet Joel became the Pentecostal outpouring of the Spirit of God. So Solomon prayed for a national restoration and revival like the pouring of rain upon parched ground, unrestricted and continuous. So let us pray for it, fulfilling the conditions before uttering the petitions.

Part 6

Prayers for the REVIVAL OF GOD'S WORK

18

Rent Heavens

'Oh that Thou wouldest rend the heavens, that Thou wouldest come down, that the mountains might flow down at Thy presence, as when the melting fire burneth, the fire causeth the waters to boil, to make Thy name known to Thine adversaries, that the nations may tremble at Thy presence!' (Isaiah 64:1, 2).

These words have always been favourite ones for preachers on revival. They also gave the title to R.B. Jones' book about the 1904-5 revival in Wales – *Rent Heavens*.

The Hebrew word 'rend' means to tear off, that is, clothes in humiliation and repentance. It was a word that could also be used of 'painting the eyes to enlarge them'! How we need to open our eyes to see what God has done in the past and is able to do in the present and future.

First, Isaiah was praying for divine perception. He was asking that heaven's curtains be drawn back so that God 'with enlarged eyes' might see the dire need for His work to be revived. In verse 4 the prophet confesses human blindness, a lack of perception of what God has done in the past. Sin had blinded their eyes as the church's have been blinded today in that we do not see that only the sovereign God can help us in our days of spiritual decline.

Isaiah could see the Holy City desolate, the land being destroyed, the people of God being carried into distant lands. If only he could persuade God to see the situation with His all-seeing eyes, through prevailing prayer, then surely God would open the gates of heaven and then descend in revival power for their help: 'O that Thou wouldest come down!'

A plea for divine perception thus becomes a prayer for divine presence. Isaiah was not asking for any army of angels, the hosts of heaven to help on God's work – THOU! God's presence alone would suffice.

Revival has been described as nothing less than 'God's presence among His people.' Not, we notice, the presence of an evangelist, a revivalist, but God Himself. Eifion Evans' title of his book describing the 1858-60 revival is *When He is Come*.

Two words stand out in Habakkuk 3:3 'God came!' Every true revival is a manifestation of the presence of God. Revival begins, continues and is consummated by God. 'The LORD alone shall be exalted in that day' (Isaiah 2:17).

In the 1904-5 revival in Wales a miner was walking home from the coal mine at 4 a.m. in the morning. He passed a chapel in which a light had been left on. The building was empty – there was no light on! He fell to his knees and said 'God is here'. He was so overwhelmed by the presence of God that he was converted on the doorstep of the church.

Duncan Campbell tells of an incident in the Hebrides revival. An irreligious Glasgow business man stepped off the boat on one of the islands of the Hebrides and was 'suddenly conscious of God'. Before he reached the main road he was a converted man. A minister of the gospel who was much involved in that revival said: 'Walking along the road or conversing with people on the hillside, one was conscious of a Presence that could not be explained from any human angle, so real, so wonderful was this sense of God.'

It is that kind of Divine presence that makes the work of God so easy to perform.

Next, Isaiah prayed for divine power.

Isaiah expected God to do certain things which only He could do: 'The mountains might flow down at Thy presence.' This is descriptive of intense heat such as an erupting volcano, the hot lava spreading out like a river in full flood. So the reviving fires of God spread into communities, churches, nations, the world, as the work of the people of God is carried on amidst revival.

The prophet also prayed that God's name might be known to His adversaries. Yes, revival is the only real way to penetrate the camps of the humanists, agnostics and atheists. Very little effect is made in communist countries by the underground church because of the bitter persecution they experience. But revival can change all that, and that is what we in other lands where we have freedom of worship must pray for. If God can cause a Welsh miner and a Glasgow business man to tremble, so He can make communist soldiers tremble at His powerful presence. He who made each blade of grass and causes them to bend in the wind can cause His wind of the Spirit to bend stubborn hearts and wills. May He soon rend the heavens and come down upon us.

19

His Work NOT Ours

'O LORD, revive Thy work in the midst of the
years, in the midst of the years make known,
in wrath remember mercy' (Habakkuk 3:2).

The prophet Habakkuk, like us, had the
disadvantage of living in days of religious decline.
God's people had departed from worship of the
one, true living God. They had become idolatrous
and divine judgment hung over them.

God always has His man for such an hour.
Habakkuk was a man of great prayer and faith.
He took hold of God and His promises. There is
not much more that we can do at such a time.

His prayer for revival is only a brief one, but
how fervent, eloquent and comprehensive. It is a
pattern prayer that has been used by generations
of Christians yearning for revival in their own
lifetime.

First, the prophet admitted his diligence: 'O
LORD, I have heard Thy speech.'

What a pity the church is not as diligent as
Habakkuk was. 'He that hath an ear, let him hear
what the Spirit saith unto the churches' is the
message in Revelation. God has a message for
His people in every generation, but we are not

always diligent in hearing it. Habakkuk means 'seer' – the burden which Habakkuk the prophet did **see**. He was a seer and a hearer. How we need to see and hear what God is able to do in our day. Habakkuk knew what God had done in days past like delivering His people out of Egypt and into the Promised Land. Would that all God's people knew what God had done during the revivals of history, but so few read and study the thrilling times of church history today.

Habakkuk had also heard because he then had to deliver God's message. 'Cry', he was told. 'What shall I cry?' The divine answer was : 'Prepare to meet Thy God.' It was a message of threatening doom with only one way of escape. He did not 'water down' the message as some dilute the gospel today. Too many in every generation have only wanted to hear 'smooth things'. Every preacher knows that when people say at the end of a service, 'I did enjoy your sermon' it means that they have not been convicted about anything in particular. Sermons are not meant to be enjoyed.

Next, Habakkuk confessed his reverence: 'I was afraid'.

We use 'fear' here in the Biblical sense of awe and reverence.

In the preceding chapter we read: 'The LORD is in His holy temple: let all the earth keep silence before Him.' Where there is no sense of awesome holiness of God there can be no revival. When Christians live as close to the world as possible, compromising, indulging in worldly things, then revival must tarry. Only a continual consciousness of the thrice-holy nature of God prepares the way for revival. Modern Christianity is so frothy, effervescent, of a candy-floss nature, that the awesomeness our forefathers felt in worship has departed.

Thirdly, the prophet placed his confidence in God: 'O LORD, revive Thy work in the midst of the years.'

When things are not going well we say: 'What can we do? How can we remedy the situation? Who can we call in?' Not so the prophet. He does not consult a brother prophet, nor call in the evangelism department or the stewardship department. It is THY work so God can revive it.

All Christian work and witness is **HIS**, not ours, so it cannot be done in **our** way, **our** time, with **our** methods.

Sunday school teachers as well as ministers and missionaries are always tempted to pray: 'Lord, prosper my work', whereas it is His. If only we realized that, we would not be so dilatory and unconscientious in our Christian service. We would not start a thing up and then allow it to fall into abeyance. We would not write such easy letters of resignation 'for personal reasons' (whatever that may mean). We would do all our

Christian work 'as unto the Lord.'

How confident Habakkuk was that God could revive 'in the midst of the years', that is immediately, not in the remote future.

Finally, Habakkuk exercised his influence: 'in wrath remember mercy.' The prophet knew that God's people should have divine anger and judgment, for idolatry deserved such punishment. But he also knew that God was merciful as well as just. His mercy is 'from everlasting to everlasting'. As their covenant-God He could not break agreement with them. So although Habakkuk could not plead any merits he could plead for mercy. So with us. We have no merits of our own, individual or corporate, but casting ourselves upon God's mercy we may expect a heaven sent revival so that His work may prosper and progress.

20

Great Power – Great Grace

'And now, Lord, behold their threatenings: and grant unto Thy servants, that with all boldness they may speak Thy word, by stretching forth Thine hand to heal; and that signs and wonders may be done by the name of Thy holy child Jesus' (Acts 4: 29, 30).

At almost any point in time there is, in some part of the world, a section of the Christian church 'threatened' by those who oppose God and His truth. The story of the underground church in Russia is an excellent example today.

There is only one thing the threatened church can do – pray! Notice to whom they prayed on this occasion – 'Lord', a rare word in the New Testament, meaning despot or ruler.

These threatening powers were despotic, but God-the-Despot was stronger than the powers-that-be who were as mere tools in His hand, for He causes even the wrath of man to praise Him.

How difficult it is for the persecuted church to do God's work, especially the fulfilling of the great commission to go into all the world and preach the gospel. Prayer is the only thing that can be done, as the New Testament church found.

First, they prayed for a divine consciousness of the cruel menace: 'And now, Lord, behold their threatenings.'

They did not ask that the threatenings be removed; nor even that they might have strength to withstand the threatenings; nor that they might be taken right out of the threatening situation. They only asked that the Lord would look down upon them. That was sufficient, for a gracious and concerned heavenly Father could not look without also taking steps to deal with the situation.

'Threatenings' has the idea of 'forbidding' behind it. They were being forbidden to preach and teach in His Name. So today Christians are forbidden to meet, hold Sunday schools, print and circulate the Scriptures. How we should pray that God will look down in mercy upon them and then take appropriate action.

Next, they prayed for a continuation of their courageous ministry: 'Grant unto Thy servants, that with all boldness they may speak Thy words.'

A daring prayer indeed! They were asking for assistance in the very activity that had brought the threatenings upon them. They had preached with boldness at the Beautiful Gate of the Temple. There was immediate hostility. They had been charged not to speak in the Name again, now they were praying for strength to do so.

How few of our neighbours and friends hear about Jesus Christ from our lips, and yet our 'threatenings' are as nothing compared with theirs (just the pointed finger at the forehead, the cold shoulder, the mocking smile or sneer). Perhaps we would be bolder if our persecution were more severe.

Thirdly, they prayed for a continuation of divine medication: 'Stretch forth Thine hand to heal.'

Not **their** healing acts but **His**. Healing is often misnamed. It is not **faith**-healing but **divine**-healing. To heal is to cure or make whole. God-in-Christ is able to deal with the whole of man, body, mind and spirit, and bring 'wholeness'.

Why is healing separated from the 'wonders and signs' following? Because Divine healing is the most effective proof of God working. It is part of the apostolic commission. A continuation of the healing ministry would help in their proclamation of the gospel, confounding the critics and convincing doubters.

Finally, they prayed for a continuation of Christ's miracles: 'That signs and wonders may be done by the name of Thy holy child Jesus.'

An alternative translation for 'child' is servant, which counteracts the Roman Catholic doctrine that the infant Jesus performed miracles before His 'ordination', His baptism in Jordan.

Their real desire in this prayer was that God's name should be vindicated and glorified. Coupled with their preaching they wanted signs of confirmation. 'Signs and wonders' is always in the plural in the New Testament, and they are always co-joined. They were the wonderful works of God that attested to His active presence among His people – the God-given credentials, the divine authenticity of the messenger.

'The day of miracles is over' says the world. 'Not so', says the true church, 'for we see them over and over again, in the conversion of sinners and in the raising up of the sick.' And when the church becomes revived we shall see more and more of these miracles, all proving the reality of the gospel we preach.

This great prayer was immediately answered: 'the place was shaken.' This proved the prayer was heard and that His power was still available. They were all filled with the Holy Spirit. It was a 'second Pentecost'. They were able to go out and preach with boldness and multitudes believed.

'Great power gave great grace' says one commentator. These are also two characteristics of the revived church – power and grace: power to preach and grace to season the preaching so that it becomes acceptable to the hearers.

21

The Greatest Revivalist

'I bow my knees unto the Father of our Lord Jesus Christ . . . that ye may be filled with all the fulness of God. Now unto Him that is able to do exceeding abundantly above all that we ask or think, according to the power that worketh in us, unto Him be glory in the church by Christ Jesus throughout all ages, world without end. Amen' (Ephesians 3:14, 19-21).

No one in Scripture was more experienced in revival blessing than the apostle Paul. He is the greatest revivalist of all time. Wherever he went he saw a movement of the Spirit of God.

He was concerned that many Christians of his time might experience it too, and so in ancient manuscripts there is a gap at the beginning of the Letter to the Ephesians – no place name is given, it was meant to be a circular letter going around to many churches. We might address it to ourselves today.

This is another model or pattern prayer for all concerned about revival today.

First, fervency was coupled with humility: 'I bow my knees unto the Father.' He is not saying that praying on our knees is the most efficacious position for prayer. It is not the position of the body that matters in prayer but the posture of the heart. In the Bible men and women prayed kneeling, standing, sitting and prostrate. It is the humility of the heart that counts with God, and then calling Him, like Paul – 'Father', the simplest form of baby speech, 'Abba' or 'Daddy'. Paul went into God's presence as humble as a child approaching his father.

Fervency is also in this prayer. Here is the picture of a courtier before his king or a beggar before his benefactor, pleading for a favour.

It is not the logic or length of our prayers; nor the Scriptural quotations incorporated; it is the strong crying with tears, the fervency and not the cold formal tone that weighs with God.

Next, Paul coupled capacity with immensity: 'That ye may be filled with all the fulness of God.'

Every believer has the capacity to be filled with the Holy Spirit, but we are not always willing. 'Filled to the measure of God's fulness' is a better translation. What immensity! Our capacity can hardly contain His immensity so there is bound to be an overflowing!

Some believe that Paul had in mind here the Shekinah-glory filling the temple. So believers are to be filled with God's fullness, all His fullness, not partial or limited, but to overflowing. The mind boggles so we can only pray, like Paul, for the experience.

Then expectancy is coupled with efficacy: 'Able to do exceeding abundantly above all that we ask or think, according to the power that worketh in us.'

Paul always prayed daring prayers. Like William Carey he 'expected' great things as well as 'attempted' great things.

How we limit our prayers to what we think God can do! True prayer is expansive, it stretches out beyond human limitations. It is not only expansive but **expensive**: it costs us in time and effort.

How can we pray as daringly as Paul? Through 'the power that worketh in us', that is, letting God Himself work above our expectations. Just as we had a foretaste of His transforming power at conversions, so we must let the same power that has **wrought** in us go on **working** in us.

Finally, majesty is coupled with eternity: 'Unto Him be glory in the church by Christ Jesus throughout all ages, world without end.'

When every Christian is living with a revived heart, exhibiting the fullness of God to all around, then the divine majesty will be seen throughout the fellowship. The church is always the instrument in the New Testament through which God's glory is manifest to the world. One day the church will be glorified, without spot or wrinkle or any such blemish. Until then we must daily become filled with God's fullness.

So while we cannot fathom all the apostle's meaning, we must be praying with holy aspiration for the experience, striving to attain this fullness, longing to be what He is. In the words of F. R. Havergal:

O fill me with Thy fullness, Lord,
Until my very heart o'erflow
In kindling thought and glowing word,
Thy love to tell, Thy praise to show.

Epilogue

22

Revival Prayers Answered by Fire

'Hear me, O LORD, hear me, that this people may know that Thou art the LORD God, and that Thou hast turned their heart back again' (1 Kings 18: 37).

THEN THE FIRE OF THE LORD FELL (v. 38).

'And David called upon the LORD' (1 Chronicles 21:26).

(GOD) ANSWERED HIM FROM HEAVEN BY FIRE (v.26).

'These all continued with one accord in prayer and supplication' (Acts 1:14).

THERE APPEARED UNTO THEM CLOVEN TONGUES LIKE AS OF FIRE, AND IT SAT UPON EACH OF THEM (2:3).

We may pray for revival, sometimes for years, regularly and fervently, and yet with little or no idea how God will answer. We expect an answer for we know God is faithful.

There are fewer and fewer Christians who have experienced revival and can tell us how God answered their prayers.

Charles Haddon Spurgeon once prayed: 'Answer us by fire, we pray Thee! Oh, for the fire to fall again – fire which shall effect the most stolid! Oh, that such fire might first sit upon the disciples, and then fall on all around!'

The above three texts make it plain. God answered by fire the prayers of Elijah, David and the disciples before the day of Pentecost.

Fire in Scripture is a metaphor for revival, as we have already seen in the previous revival prayers. But why is fire also the way God answers? It stands, like water, for cleansing (see Isaiah 6: 6,7). It is symbolic, like water, for life, and like light it can stand for judgment. But it is unique in standing for God's presence (Genesis 15:17 and Exodus 3:2, for example). And we have already seen that revival is nothing less than God's presence.

Now these three texts of our epilogue contain three common elements:

First, the source of the fire.

It was a divine source: 'The fire of the Lord' . . . 'HE. . . answered by fire' . . . 'I will pour out'.

Revival is always a vindication of God's honour and in an extraordinary manner, letting mankind know that He is sovereign and supreme. A God-consciousness occurs just as the light from heaven fell upon Saul of Tarsus on the Damascus road.

109

In England the fireplace has always been the focal point of a family's living room, and even in modern days of central heating usually an artificial fire is incorporated to give a similar effect. So the focal point in every revival is the fire of God, a fire that spreads, consumes, cleanses and convicts.

In unrevived times the church is only lukewarm, like the church of Laodicea. A lukewarm church is hypocritical, it gives the impression of zeal and spirituality but it denies it in practice. A cold church can be warmed up, there is hope for it, so the Lord likes a cold church rather than a lukewarm one which He would 'spue' out of His mouth. In reality God loves a boiling hot church, and since He is the source of revival fire He alone can make us white-hot with passionate love and zeal for the lost and for one another. We must make it our prayer: 'Come as the fire; and purge our hearts like sacrificial flame.'

Next, note **the direction of the fire** – from above.

For Elijah the fire fell. For David it came from heaven, as it did for the disciples on the day of Pentecost.

From above, yet all the while we look around for the solution to our spiritual troubles and declension. We look to men and methods; we look to bigger and better publicity; we try the latest visual aid and call in the audio aids experts. And the more we look around the busier we become. The more we organize instead of agonizing in prayer, the more we try instead of trusting the sovereign God of revival. How we need to pray, remembering the direction of the fire:

Come, Holy Ghost, in love,
Shed on us from above
Thine own bright ray.

Or

Come down, O Love Divine,
Seek Thou this soul of mine,
And visit it with Thine own ardour glowing;
O Comforter, Draw near,
Within my heart to appear,
And kindle it,
Thy holy flame bestowing.

Finally, note **the purpose of the fire** – revival!

For Elijah, God turned back the people's hearts; for David, he was enabled to proceed with the plans for the temple; for the disciples in the upper room, three thousand were converted and added to the church on the day of Pentecost.

This is God's purpose for us today, right up to the return of Christ. We are not to become content with less. Certainly we are not to 'despise the day of small things,' but neither are we meant to be content with them either. 'There remaineth yet much land to be possessed.' The world is teeming with lost souls going to a Christless eternity.

There is much talk about preparing for revival. It is not preparing (through this method or that method) but pleading. God is looking for pleaders, mighty intercessors, prayer-warriors. If we base our prayers upon the models and patterns and examples contained in Holy Scripture then our prayers must prevail and they will be answered by the God who answers by fire.